THE PACIFIC NORTHWEST POETRY SERIES

Linda Bierds, General Editor

THE PACIFIC NORTHWEST POETRY SERIES

Republic CAFE

DAVID BIESPIEL

UNIVERSITY OF WASHINGTON PRESS

Seattle

Republic Café, the nineteenth volume in the Pacific North-
west Poetry Series, is published with the generous support of
Cynthia Lovelace Sears.

Copyright © 2018 by the University of Washington Press
Printed and bound in the United States of America
Design by Katrina Noble
Composed in Scala, typeface designed by Martin Majoor
Jacket background photograph by Jacob Stephens on Unsplash
22 21 20 19 18   5 4 3 2 1

UNIVERSITY OF WASHINGTON PRESS
www.washington.edu/uwpress

LIBRARY OF CONGRESS CATALOGING-IN-PUBLICATION DATA
Names: Biespiel, David, 1964– author.
Title: Republic Café / David Biespiel.
Description: Seattle : University of Washington Press, [2018] | Series: The
    Pacific Northwest poetry series |
Identifiers: LCCN 2018046909 (print) | LCCN 2018051154 (ebook) | ISBN
    9780295744544 (ebook) | ISBN 9780295744537 (hardcover : alk. paper)
Subjects: LCSH: American poetry—21st century.
Classification: LCC PS3552.I374 (ebook) | LCC PS3552.I374 R47 2019 (print) |
    DDC 811/.54—dc23
LC record available at https://lccn.loc.gov/2018046909

For WRW

To live your life is not as simple as to cross a field.
—BORIS PASTERNAK

The empire is nothing but a zodiac of the mind's phantasms.
—ITALO CALVINO

The pleasures of heaven are with me, and the pains of hell are with me.
—WALT WHITMAN

CONTENTS

ROOM

After it came in like a dark bird
Out of the snow, barely whistling
The notes *father, mother, child,*
It was hard to say what made us happiest.

Seeing the branches where it had learned
To stir the air? The air that opened
Without fear? Just the branches
And us in a room of wild things?

Like a shapeless flame, it flew
A dozen times around the room.
And, in a wink, a dozen more.
Into the wall, the window, the door.

You said the world turns to parts.
You said the parts are cunning spheres.
You said you always love the face of sin.
You said it's here, the lips and eyes and skin.

Outside the snow deepened
With heaves of discontent.
Inside, the tremor of our life
Flew in and in and in.

REPUBLIC CAFÉ

1

We are walking home and the sun is high,
And coming alongside us on the street in our city is the drone
    of a truck.
The city is a streaming procession of early summer green, with
    light behind the hills rising and luring us into its smoke.

You are talking about the white flowers that are blossoming.

Watching you in your blue dress, I think—
She has the look of a woman dizzy with the love of wide petals
    and rivers,
And she is ready to sit down and rest on the banks where a few
    children are tossing a ball,
And the water is sparkling with their shouts.
There are splashes from birds and fish, and a revving of boats.

If you ask me what is the shape of the world,
I would say it's a spiral, a cone, a wisp of smoke
Spinning on the long axis of remembering and forgetting.
A balustrade, fractal, strand of genetic instruction.

But I have not yet established my orientation,
Nor am I ready to follow the smoke.

The shape of the world is a wreath of alliances, promises,
    despair that leads to terror,
Times of day and night when one knows where north and
    south are,
Like a garland of rangeland fencing.

When I was a boy, north was the Red River.

———

Sometimes, in this meager journal, I am I. Other times, he.
Full of God, you are always you, and you are always she.

———

But it's as if morning doesn't want to begin again,
And so in trying to bring it back,

As if from the surface of a cave
Shaped like a skull,

To bring back moments of survival
Before the first catalogs of light appear,

I grope for what feels like scratches on the hollow of a thigh,
Like seeing ashen clouds zipper across the sky.

2

It's not true that I forget things, the memories are there,
Slanted like a fingernail,
And they exist before anything else
At the beginning of the story.
The imprecision of it is what is most precise.

It's like toppling face down over gravel and feeling that all I'll
   remember is the falling, the sharpness.

———

In this room, I am oriented by the river to the west
And mountains to the east.
Farther off are the puzzle pieces of America with its gentle
   rogues and vistas and easy dollars and protests.

———

Beyond, there's the splotchy disappearance
And exactitudes of Europe and Arabia,
Where the deserts of the prophets are sometimes sandstone
   and other times sand,
The deserts not barren lands
But behind each hill and each valley is a man who does not
   look for God within him

So sure that he is within God—

It's a place for visions,
Even the ground seems only focused on the sky
With the wild geese honking like herds of goats
Shepherded by Bedouins
Who stop to look at clumps of box thorn that twist in the sand
    like a coronet of barbed wire.

From here I get the news of the world.
I map and intersect the grid lines of what I have yet to forget.
In this way, everything remains where it is all at once, and I
    remember almost nothing.
Like a shadow of rain clouds in the sky's mouth,
Everything that appears, disappears.

3

In a city neither was born in, we are nameless.
After making love, we are ash.

Studded into the folds and embrace of an elbow, my sweat is
    like dust.
In the folds of your elbows, down to your wrists, your skin
    glitters
Like first stars.

––––––––

I put these down as memorandums—
A woman will place her heart into the palm of a man, I say, a
    man into the palm of a woman.
In the ruin of a human heart, you say, a heart will rot like a
    piece of fruit.

––––––––

Tomorrow I must write: *The imprint of a shadow of a leaf on the
    dark ground is God protecting all of us.*

4

Nothing had told me love meant dragging the dead across
    the hills.

———

Holding your body was like coming in from a village under
    papery skies
And gathering there, along the road, a basketful of berries.
Later the fruit withers or gets plowed in,
And a small fire will keep the room shuttered.

———

From the beginning you expect the love to go badly.
From the beginning you touch the fables in our skin.

5

Clouds like a white dog lying on its back with its paws pointed
  upward,
Clouds like jets blurring in flight,
Clouds like a lonely man wrestling with doubt where hope
  is pushed against a bare tree and people sleep in the
  dirty streets.

————

We are sinners who know there are factories in the dark, and
  meadows in the dark.

————

The clouds are no surprise.
Danger and suffering do not always astonish us.

6

Love wears a porcelain bracelet with a crow on it.
Love dresses in a smoky kimono and dances in our room.

———

What are these velvety clouds
Streaming by like a new religion?

———

Can the crow use its beak to restore the blank faces of the dead?
Can its eyes find the ghost we are seeking that can unite the
    colors of sunlight with the stories of brightness that fade in
    the white skies of the afternoon,
The relics of childhood with the pieces of our minds,
The languages we have forgotten with the calling of who we are?

7

Like the sun rising in the broken morning—as if in a trance—
The blue morning the World Trade Center is attacked is
    cloudless as the day Hiroshima was bombed.

Even that day as we watch the morning not yet begun, far
    across America in the West,
I feel suddenly in my memory that it's also six days into the
    fall of 1805—
And over tide breaks near Astoria the Columbia River spills its
    waters into the ocean
And William Clark and his corps are exposed in the dismal
    notch to the mercy of the waters
And the hard rains and the floods and immense waves and
    heavy winds
And floating two-hundred-foot trees
And the drifts that threatened the canoes,
And it takes all attention to save the canoes from the timbre of
    trees that crumpled right out of the floors of the earth,
Trees, like the sides of houses, seven feet wide,
And every man wet as water could make them—
A right disagreeable situation, says Clark,
Cold and wet, and bullet-shaped stones falling upon them, too.

Just then, from the other side of the river, like ghosts,
The Cathlama are paddling in their canoes easily across the
    highest waves ever seen,
The Cathlama scattering their canoes like silence—
Those Indians are Certainly—William Clark writes—*the best
    Canoe navigaters I ever Saw.*

Followed by more hard claps of thunder.
Followed by balls of hail, and for a short time, a little light,
    then violent rains,
All wet and cold, and the bedding, too.

————

Tomorrow I must write: *The wounded and the living stumble into
    joy, but the body's sweetness is natural.*

————

After the endless repetitions
And blistering skin of war
Come the tourists.

In one exhibition, you can see narrow stairs and strobe lights.
Hanging from the ceiling are plastic mushroom clouds with
    effigies of vapor and debris and low-density gas,
With stem end and smoke end—
Above Hiroshima the mushroom cloud went forty-five
    thousand feet up as a bubble of after-wind.

If you were to fly in an airplane that high,
Below you would see a white desert of sinking canyons
And hills and ravines of clouds
And the horizon flattening into a blue rim.

In Nagasaki the death morning was perfectly clear,
The rock gardens silent and fastidious.

From the east came a flash
Like a bright membrane of some other sky.

For the sake of forgetting, I write:
Dispersal and scatter and drift and splintering of dust.

Later, the love of being
Followed by a stain.

8

The day the World Trade towers fall was bright as the day
  Hiroshima was bombed.
People were going to work inside the rubble of their bodies,
  shops were just beginning to open, orchids of bells tingled
  against the glass doors.
Children were in schools.

———

In both, a new weapon is brought into our lives.
In both, the dust is in our mouths.

In one, a new world power comes forward, while in the other,
  we cease for a time to be what Walt Whitman calls "the
  greatest poem."

———

As now, too, when the sun is done rising over the west, done
  with its ritual chords of blueing the air, there will be some
  who love,
There will be some who do not mean harm, there will be some
  who are innocent, there will be some who are baffled,
  there will be some who are tender.

9

Tomorrow I must write: *Just ahead is the empty street with all the names of the dead.*

───────

Here I am—in white gowns, in hospital hallways—
Say the men and women who shuffle their feet to the music of broken glass.

───────

Same as them, we've arrived in this room secretly,
As the high windows square off against the soft rain.

Without memory, all we can see is the diorama of our lives
    across thousands of miles among silk fans and small
    pillows
And blinds over the windows that let in some forgotten light
    that was torn from the afternoon.

10

This journal is an alphabet for the glare of trees in heavy
    sunlight,
The past that lights the lamps and, in the shine of the old
    songs,
Rattles and bares its teeth.

There will be screaming in the beginning and calling the
    names of the years softly,
Crushed hours dissolving against the night,
Undressed bodies mouthing through the crack of a door,
Blossoms, like a last memory, come down out of the blue skies
Burned into them.

———

The words I write are common.
The words I don't write swell and stand away from the other
    words.

———

If the unseen is to be seen,
It must be the one place in creation that is spiraling
    languidly—

Like the end of the road where a few faces come into view out
of the heap—
So that tomorrow, at daybreak, the light will be deposited into
the throng of my book.

11

This is a journal about the corpses of war.

After a bombing, after a sneak attack,
The men and women who survive do not become like
    stray dogs.
But still they belong to no one.
Their skin is cold as rain.
Their loves cannot be remembered.
Whether lost, whether old,
Or, as they are, stripped to their night clothes in hospitals,
They have become mild,
Since the danger of poison is passed,
And they turn their backs toward wisdom
As if living among rocks and weeds.

————

This is in Hiroshima.
This is in Manhattan.

————

Nurses in the hospital climb the stairs.
The candlelight vigils go on throughout the chalky nights.

Men climb step by step in the hospital before resting in a
    small chair
Just as the Lord sits with the dead watching darkness sweeten
    the fall crops.
But the dead have not decided if they are lonely.

At two a.m. or at three a.m. or four, at five a.m., there are
    only questions:
Do the dead wonder what this man will do to that woman?
Do the dead remember getting old?
The times they saw nothing?
Being poor? Or getting by?
Do they ask for balance and clarity, or emotional fantasy, or
    absence of tonality and structure, or the exotic?
Do the dead prefer Brahms? Or John Philip Sousa?

When the sea fades with the daily tides, and the memories are
    finished, where do the dead sit?
What words come to their blue tongues?
Do the dead say, we are fine.

And the Lord, where will the Lord sit?
And the nurses, where will they sit?

12

In our hidden room, onto my bare shoulders, you lightly
    scrawl the word *you*.
Three letters step over a flat, grassy field across the big pools
    of shadows the clouds make and then straddle the hills
    and horizon
And, with a procession of mouths, speak of what's beyond the
    unknown.

———

Your voice dwindles like a whistle to companions—
You are lying on your side, your head propped on a blue pillow.
You say, pain in the world exists side by side with desire in
    the world.

You say, we are catastrophes,
Nourished by black feathers
And two eyes that no longer return a new light.

———

I say, it's like we've undressed inside an unread novel
Where the hours are softly darkening,
And we wonder whether life is going on in the other rooms.

13

Imagine a model city the size of a drawing room—
There would be a model river and model bridges and model
   windmills and model schools and model desks.
Imagine yearning and rejoicing and waking up happy with
   your ancient joys,
With a grandfather in the furrows of the low garden, calipering
   the hedges,
As pink blossoms fall over his eyes.

Now remember the war when some were cold and poor and
   others were not,
When there were vacant streets there and crowded shops here,
When the bombs fell like glints of petals over the early weeks
   of the new century.

———

Who remembers the sight of the bare legs of schoolchildren
   as they wander in museums, of fifteen-foot-long airplanes
   hanging from the ceiling,
Or the pressed blouse and white gloves of the tour guide with
   her ice-cream cap and microphone,
Bright smile, and the sound of her laughter like weeping?

———

When the sirens started below the World Trade Center, when
    the metal was twisted, when the massive waves arrived,
    when the river was forded, when the doctor was still a boy,
When the bulbs were underground, when the famous imitated
    the famous, when the sadness became permanent,
When the foolish turned in beds,
When the exaggerations became absurd, when fat lies were
    made into songs of war,
When keys snapped in the locks,
When small fish felt for the bottom sand, when wonder turned
    to envy, when the shrieks were a bouquet of bees,

He was in the American West
Where her austerity seemed to him like a broken bicycle,
And they lay down together inside the belly of the night
Under the clearest skies either had ever seen.

14

Late autumn witness—
Love is hard to relinquish just as a little valley of sun is.
It's like flowers for a bride's wrist,
Flowers for a grave under a tree at the side of a road.

———

In my two green eyes are your green eyes.
We both see the burning city of Rome, the eternal city,
Where there is the trial of raging against the anointed.
The brute Romans, and their hypocrite emperors, and their
    lust for spectacle
Provide us so much generosity in their errors and faded tenors
    of glory.
Inside my teeth are the end days after the emperor has
    abandoned his era of conquest,
After Hannibal departs the city, having come over the Pyrenees
And the crowns of the Alps with his war elephants,
And the Roman citizens trampled across the crevasses of the
    little bridges,
And their roseate bodies, found later on the painted ceilings,
Are like most bodies
Patched together with bare flesh, and scars and tissue, and
    hair fallen out of their heads.

———

Memory is the underpaintings of despair pressed like half thoughts onto the flypaper of books.

15

All that I've forgotten can be seen from my window as
    shattered glass falling out of the Manhattan skies
And people pausing to catch their breaths at Cortland Street.

————

There was an intercom with a voice.
Above Bloomingdale's, a jet.

————

There was putting out both hands blindly to feel for the side of
    a building through the falling ash.

16

Just as when Hannibal arrives in triumph in Rome with the
    avenues deserted and the weeds undefeated,
Through Times Square, a police escort of semis with digging
    equipment on flatbeds arrives from the iron mines of
    Minnesota.

————

What was I thinking of when I saw a burned bald spot in one
    man's head as a map of Crimea,
The rest of his small head as the Black Sea?
I was thinking, between suffering is what God wants.

————

I witnessed nothing.
Love glittered like a blue marble rolled across a bridge.

17

Even now, tightening inside my testicles decades after the
    exterminations camps,
There is dust on the roads, and the grass is dull.
Clouds the color of rope.

Whatever the name of the town, it is a town of barracks,
The wood sidings pleasant, the insides efficiently cool with
    concrete,
And the benches provide a place to put down clothes.

There are the windowless bathhouses.
Spy hole in the door.
Naked men and naked women and the children naked,
Then hot air with pale blue crystals of gas—

What need to scrawl on the floor with chalk the word *Vergast?*

———

The barges of time cross with blue eyes.

I am not ashamed to know things, and I know that television
    is nothing like memory
With its alternations of snow and sleet and the roads glazed.

In the reconstruction on television
The events are always in the same order.
Sky, jets, fires,
Until the screen cuts or darkens
And the broadcaster resumes, or takes a break,
And a commercial pops up for hair removal product.

The reconstruction on television makes apocalyptic freaks look
    like symmetrical adversaries.
The reconstruction on television confuses the real with the
    symbolic and makes murder look like a spectacle of the
    sublime.

———

In memory there is something to do with archways under a
    bright sky, the aroma of high cotton.
Straw in the wind.

18

Always there is the last survivor climbing out of the rubble,
And buildings like gashes of great mouths with blue tongues
    hanging open.

————

Isn't it easiest to see the other side of one's own death
When the wind goes on and on
And the mouth closes,
And the skulls whiten,
And the afterlife, like rain, falls in the trees,
And the pink flesh of daylight shatters the splendor of the
    windows,
And the far-off fire is white
When it burns on the oily water,
And the women and men are saving themselves in the low
    tides of the bay
And death clings to whatever skin is there?

————

When I say forgetting, I mean reconstructing the soft winds
    that come with sweetness in the mornings.

19

There comes a scream through a dark house.
A man's face stares out of the newsreel,
His teeth white as the pages of a new book.
While lamps flutter and the mist goes black,
He rushes in all directions to dodge the fire, waving his arms,
As if seeing God for the first time.

———

He had been standing on a car hood under the filthy sky
Waving his arms all along,
His legs emaciated like fine thread,
And turning in half circles,
Like a street sweeper without a broom.
There were scars above his cheek,
Flowery bruises,
Flies in the nostrils,
Gnats in the branches like shadows of air.

If he is praying with hands clasped,
If he seems to be eating a slice of bread,
If a red leaf spurts across the boulevard,
He opens his mouth toward the filthy sky,
Trying not to move too much,

Trying not to unfeel his feelings,
Nor to forget that he is forgetting.

———

Wasn't it worth it, I suppose he thinks, to have once had his
heart broken?

20

We searched for the sparse
Sky unrolling its white blossoms to the wind.

———

Men and women came to the edge of the windowsills of
    Tower One
As if to put out a cigarette
And leapt from the exploded windows.

———

Like a discarded coat, a slipper—
Twirling and flipped, and flailed, unfolding,
Gone, and blessed, and closed-eyed.

21

All that I have forgotten is smoothed into this bedspread
    underneath us, including the muddy, glistening, flattened
    city of Hiroshima in September 1945
Where a graph of rivers yearns to live in peace outside history.
The fields are gray as the eyes of a father,
And the thinning hair that has come to his head.
Where there was a house is now no more a house,
But the chopped down forelegs of trees.

———

Later the Japanese couple that lived there sold the land to an
    Englishman who converted to Shinto.
He began to carry small stones into the garden.
He became like God glittering behind his masks,
Like ash on the tongue.
In time, he avoids the questions of good and evil
And will likely no longer be confused about those things.

———

Like a red blouse drifting in the air toward the East River,
God said—Genesis 1:24—*Let the earth bring forth the living*
    creatures.

I write—

I will not be afraid of ten thousands of people—Psalm 3:6—

That have set themselves against me round about.

22

We make love as if we have never met.

You like to wrap your arms behind my back when I am lying
    above you.
Your hand rests on my shoulder and touches my warm skin
As if folding a love letter
In which you have assured me you will stay
Each night and each dawn.

In the letter we are walking near the Luxembourg Gardens,
Having left Place de Contrescarpe for our apartment on Rue
    de L'Eperon.
You want to get to the postal station in time to send the letter
    that night
But stop outside to look up at the crows landing on the rain
    gutters of the apartments.
Your wedding ring softens like the spring trees.

You say, they seem to be longing for other crows.
I say, and old rivers.

———

As when a paper ferry crosses a paper lake in a hush of paper
    mountains,

And the paper passengers forget their mouths,
And paper fireworks blossom and plunge in the skies
And are over in a moment
Like the strata that cross the earth,

So, too, we shuffled under the feeble air and savored the hurt
    of all our previous nights.

————

You show me your palm,
Your love lines like smoke drifting through the room.
I see children who danced their way up into the night sky,
Lightheaded from hunger, who disappeared—
But even now one is looking back like a falling star,
And all the others who reached the sky are a band of coyotes
    dancing.

23

When the fish died after Hiroshima,
They were lined up by the silvery thousands and had to be
    thrown into the dump.
When the fish died, fear became an object one couldn't bury.
When the fish died, no one was thinking of ideas.

The protest marches lasted for months.
The citizens marched in the salvaged streets and shouted into
    bullhorns.
The protestors raised red-and-white posters depicting dead fish.

———

Above them the skies were clear.
The clouds were poor pilgrims gone missing.

———

But should a beautiful girl come into the path of the
    demonstrators with her school friends, she might be
    saying something else entirely,
That time defends her, that she intends to grow old.

24

We awake in the cloud-filled hours with puddles of water
stained on the asphalt.

———

Buoyed, in the middle of the room, we are like a small boat
alone on the water.

———

History sighs in the open sea.

25

There are those, I say, who die for us every day.
What a horrible sacrifice, you say, this freedom without
    beginning that should save us.

———

Where I'm from, I say, the garments of the damned are still
    clicking
In the windstorms and mesquite prairies.

———

In time we shall be nourished with unending fullness
And with the invisible mornings of our hymns, I say.
You say, we shall be nourished with trees of black feathers.

26

You say, look, there are miles of smoke cooling through your
    shirt, feeling for your throat.

———

We understand this to mean that another city must be burned
    down,
And the soundless ashes, scattered and misbegotten, are the
    color of our lips.

———

You say, and then forgiveness?

27

Decades after the survivors are saved from the death camps,
    they will give testimony in accents few people still
    understand.
Even now, heading into another war,
We know that mothers and children will be driven from their
    homes.
At every stage of the new war, the police will threaten, and
    they'll say, if you come here again, we'll shoot you.
The underground movement will hide her children in
    orphanages with money from the Red Cross until the
    liberation.
Then, there will be nowhere to go.

———

We know after some midnight, the soon-to-be-dead will be
    shoved from trains—*Raus! Schnell!*—and we know a guard
    will say, *Leave your luggage, you'll get it later.*
The old and sick will be thrown from the trains into the
    ditches,
And others will shove out quickly, with pushing and hitting.

When the dogs bark,
Nobody will say a word.

The men will be separated from the women,
Thousands lined up
Like tracks of stunted birds in the sand.

But a mother standing with her three sisters tries to escape the
     women's line
To find her son, to say something to him.
A dog is barking at her legs—
And she senses a rifle pointed at her,
And now she's found her little boy in one of the lineups.
But the mother is quickly being pulled back.

We know up ahead another baby will be taken from her
     mother.
No, she protests—as a guard hits her in the cheek—
No, you cannot have my baby!

She is trying to stand, her elbow bruised from the fall.
The guard is giving the baby to a stranger in line and says to
     that man, *Take this baby.*
The guard hits the mother again, this time with the butt of a
     rifle, this time in the ribs.
The dog's teeth show through wrinkled, black lips,
And its handler is struggling with the lead.
But the mother wants her baby.
So finally the guard shoves her to the right into the other line
To die with the baby.
He had wanted her in the line to the left, where she would
     have lived.
But, no, she wants to go with the baby.

———

Tomorrow I must write: *Already I am forgetting the first body to be recovered from the debris.*

28

All in all, Rome collapsed under its own weight.

———

After the mob killed the emperor, the system of generals and
   senators splintered into warlords,
And the history of Europe was set in place for two millennia.

In the First Crusade—in 1099—thirteen thousand crusaders
   after three years and three thousand miles marching
   arrived in June at the gates of the city where Jesus of
   Nazareth died.
The Christians captured a Muslim defender, strapped him
   to a catapult, and flung him like a missile back over the
   high walls,
And the Muslims counterattacked with pots of oil and flaming
   bolts.
After the crusaders breached the walls, they slaughtered thirty
   thousand Muslims, Jews, and fellow Christians.

———

In our room, we are amateurs at pleasure—
You pull the weight of my body, like an incantation, closer.

29

You kiss the center of my chest as if writing another beautiful
    love letter.
Each night and each dawn are written with lavender ink on
    white paper to get my loyalty and affection.
With each kiss you finish off another letter.

———

Your green eyes are the cities the letters cross over to reach me.

———

I rub my fingers through your words as if touching the feet of
    children running in panic.

30

Because the past travels distances—downstream and out of
   sight to where the water is dark and easy and the sun
   bursts and the grass dies in late summer
And the small trees are no longer in blossom—
I find a place under the skies to disappear on the far edges of
   the horizon
Where a long train is crossing the ranchlands: a short horn-
   blast followed by three longer blasts.

———

That's the way it should be, you say, sitting straight up on the
   bed, narrow as a statue.

———

I say, what I remember is, I've spent my life knowing nothing.

31

Your past glares like sunlight on stone houses.
It's a winter past and freezes in the dark,
A past that scatters in bright windows.

———

Your past dreams of opened shop windows.

———

To remember love, we must wince against the weak sun.

You unbutton your dress
And whisper, one by one, words that slip into sleep in the
    outward land,
Newborn, courtyard, husband, promise.

32

Tomorrow I must write: *In the palm of every man's hand is the blood of war.*

———

Tomorrow I must write: *The soul is emptied like a clear day just after rain when the wind has died and the afternoon train never arrives.*

———

To be shorn of the past, I say, is to believe that each previous
    love was a mistake.
Everyone forgets—I say, leaning forward in a chair
While you are standing near the window—
It's like coming to the end of a triumph but seeing it as failure.

33

We do a lot of things out of fear, she says, just to survive.
She turns from the window.

———

Did you know, he says, in the Book of Life, when you find a
    name with a dot, the dot means there's a survivor.
You see very few dots.

———

Like little boats ready to head home, the crows are gathering
    outside the room under the old trees.
Do you think, she says, when we die they'll gather for us?

34

What did 9/11 mean to you? he asks.
The beginning of the new war, she answers,
And the beginning of indifference.

———

She was facing a mirror,
Applying lipstick.

Have you rejoiced? he asks.

She doesn't answer at first, but her eyes, through the mirror,
Look in his direction.

In the room are spirits pressing through the door
Like a bell somewhere down the road they can almost hear.

But the bell is too silent,
Even the closer it gets to them.

———

At last she answers, her eyes inside the smudged bevels of glass,
Why do we always go over what we should have done, and not
    what we did?

35

He says, it's impossible to know who will see our disguises
    as something other than pieces of broken stone destroyed
    years ago.

————

She is taking off her shoes, letting her hair down,
Looking absently at the floor.

————

When you see bird tracks on the shoreline, he tells her, they
    are like the handwriting of God.
The tracks in the sand cannot be forgotten, he says, and
    cannot be remembered.

But the birds forget the tracks, she says.
It's best to leave behind something to remind you where you
    have been, she says.

He says, and what should we leave behind?

She says, a photograph.
She says, we must always be in training to die.

He says, isn't our future like a drawer in a cabinet?
When the drawer opens, there will be no reason to lie to each
    other.
When the drawer closes,
We will at last open our souls to terror

Like passing the corridors and alcoves and foyers
To a new room.

36

They are sitting on the bed, folding into each other like a piece
    of paper tucked in between a door and a doorpost.
Cobbles of clouds lash against the city,
But there was no rain yet.

———

Across the street, scrawled placards from the parade read—

DON'T GLORIFY MURDERS OF 3,000
PLANES CRASH GOD LAUGHS
9-11—GIFT FROM GOD

———

The clouds arrange to meet in the middle of the sky like lovers,
And then part, so that forgetting about clouds becomes a new
    pattern against the dead.

Now the clouds are a parade of flickering light above the city
Like portraits of the missing.

37

I am not afraid, she says.

———

The parade goes on with deformed hands and burned faces
    and bleeding tongues,
Children with chicken hats, an elderly gentleman with a
    marble smile.
And the sound of marching on gravel.

———

He says, our love is a river at night crossing under a bridge.

38

At last, the ghost we were seeking all along stood before me
    like an illumination.

————

At first I thought it was a crow,
But it was a woman descending a spiral staircase from an
    orange sky
To hover near my eyes
Like a star.

She grabbed my right hand, seized my arm, kicked at my
    head.
I tackled her from the waist, tugging on her black gown.

————

Forehead to forehead, we tasted each other's name.

39

Someone was calling the ghost away,
As if calling a small girl in from the yard.

———

Calling her with a story of impossible love.

———

There was dying somewhere, despair somewhere,
Longing somewhere.

40

Desire is a conspiracy, I say—
We are both sitting under the window as the trees whiten in
    the night.

Desire causes two to be in defiance.
Two to be released from the pain of the world, two—
In the space of their own presence—
To be exempted.
Two, always, to threaten to vanish.

————

Speaking of past loves becomes our lament.

————

There is a fog in my body I never touch, I say, a black weave, a
    blot of gray air,
No matter how far down my hand reaches
Into memory's blood-rush

And death by fire.

41

We are on the bed with our palms upturned.
The sky slopes down to the river like a scar.
A few boats are lined up near one of the bridges.
From time to time, you can see candlelight in a window,
And the silence that arrives with candlelight.

———

In the crick in my neck are the Jews arriving in Grodno
    in 1039,
But in 1942 are informed that, no, none of us would be going
    to our deaths.

In the pinch of skin behind my two ears are country blossoms,
Pale stumps and uprooted weeds,
And the light of anointment that we look away from
In the waterfall of our pleasure.

———

The constellation Orion has followed me every step of my life.
Under its bow and arrow, my body has come and gone.

42

A few birds were lined up near one of the bridges in the blush
    of ordinary time.
The river bobbed under a shawl of clouds.

The air was like a testimonial of bodies lined up dead one next
    to the other,
Floating along the last curve of a road outside the village
Where sons, who no longer shrug at the sunset, lie dead
    beside their fathers,
And daughters beside their mothers among the rainy
    blossoms.

One survivor has written—
Single men picked out women from the group to be their "wives."
The rest were killed.
I was selected by a widower who took me with him into exile.
When the man was killed, I was two months pregnant.
The child was born in the refugee camp.

———

From an upturned hand, God pries a note from a father:
If anyone sees my son, tell him to take revenge.

———

So against death living becomes the son's wreath, his ceremony, his engraving.

43

We wrinkle into a large booth at the Republic Café,
Clumsy as people getting off a train,
Bumping against each other with our arms and legs.

———

Underneath the linoleum table
Where our feet graze and touch in the late afternoon
Your shoulder bag pulses against my satchel.

Whiskey, please, red wine.

———

Who's to say we didn't fly here across a yellow sky above the
    city?
Who's to say you weren't reclining in the wind, arms
    outstretched, and your dark hair pinned up with secrets
    of immortality?

44

The café is empty except for a couple of women—they're
    drunk—and the waiters.

We are like two faiths drawing near to each other.
Where the faiths meet is where we can see each other, if only
    we avoid knowing ourselves.

———

How can anybody, you say, endure such pain?
I say, if there is a soldier's body bleeding in the street, only the
    sky can know it.

———

But the sky is silent, you say.
A few swallows cooing, I say, that's all.
In that moment your eyes are like a house
Being cleared out and emptied,
And the light is weak, like the inside of a memory,
That keeps surprising us at swirling moments
When something is given back
We didn't know was ours, and with immense joy.

45

You lean forward in the booth and rest your hands across the
    dry table and describe a man crossing a blacktop.

From this distance of years,
The man is more like a boy, the marriage to another woman
    has neither begun nor yet ended.

All around him are the low inhabited buildings of a town.
As I listen to you, he seems to me to be blending into blue
    morning air.
He did not know this would happen to you when you first met,
    just the two of you back then.
Later you are riding bicycles very fast down a long hill and
    then up a steep incline across a meadow near a river.
The woods are deep like a stillness that attends death,
And you are ducking under stray branches on your bicycles,
Breathing hard the way one does when they are young and in
    love for the first time.

I describe a woman in a white blouse and blue jeans sitting in
    a chair, her legs crossed, and her voice like the blossom of
    vines on the shady side of a house.

She would like to become pregnant with her husband who often
     waits for her like a sentinel on their porch late at night.
She fills the whole world with her ripeness and likes to speak
     of ruins and the way that winter trees waver like the sound
     of the ocean inside a shell.

———

What do you think about to preserve memory? you ask.
Falling petals? Names and dates of the dead? Broken mirrors?
     Past loves?

I say, memories are a smokestack in search of a sky.
I say, memories are a boy walking under the trees.
I say, memories are visible when burned underground.
I say, memories are sand in a dream with a strong wind.

You say, why speak of some loves, and not others.

46

The drunk couple is kissing, and the waiters have disappeared
   for what seems like an hour.
It is dark, and the lamplight hardly stirs.
Outside there's a little rain and the windows are covered with
   midges.
A day will come when the living and the dead will change
   places.

———

Somewhere in our lives, as if we are always hiding in a stone
   cellar
With soldiers marching past,

Where one's hands feel like the shadows of trees in silence,
There remains an unsolved love.

It's like living in a constant state of emergency
Where home is what we carry in our bodies and not an
   address.

It's as if we are clawing at the saltpeter in the walls until our
   fingers bleed,
And we are sucking the bloody fingers.

In the Republic Café I am sitting with a light heart.
Outside there are little bundles of rain in the grass
And the birds are quivering in their cloaks.

As in a dream the air is red near the horizon
And orange at the rooftops
And a tree ripples with the music of a violin

That quiets, as if shuddering, atop the roof of a brown house,
While below a blind woman in a purple skirt holds a white fan,
Saying somewhere in our knuckles is the taste of blood.

47

I have seen this before.

———

I remember how in Alain Resnais's *Hiroshima mon amour*—
The Japanese is a man who is happy with his wife.
The French woman is a woman who is happy with her
   husband.

They are in his room in the city of Hiroshima.
His wife is out of town, and they have met the night before.

It would have been too easy, the Japanese says,
When he learns later that the French woman is leaving for
   Paris by plane in the morning.

The whole thing is ridiculous, the French woman says.

It is not yet evening, a white sky, and the phone keeps
   ringing—they embrace, followed by kissing.
She's looking at nothing over his shoulder except at her own
   thoughts of herself in this moment.
It is for the sake of looking only, her looking is.

———

In her eyes is the understanding that Paris is liberated
And Hiroshima is again a living city—

And even the bars, where they met the night before—
But you don't know this yet—are open late with jukeboxes and
    glasses of Sapporo.
They have both survived, and their pain with their joy is who
    they have become.

They are almost pressed against a bookshelf now,
But no longer embracing exactly, her wedding ring on her
    right hand like a slender silence against the ringing of the
    telephone.

She is unbuttoning her white blouse in front of him.
Her eyes are brightening and have the look of looking
As her fisted hand, one by one, fingers the buttons

And the top of her blouse opens—
She asks, *What difference can it make?*

She doesn't mean to be offhand.
She's asking, what difference can it make?

48

Outside the window, a crow rattles into the slot
And trickles down the chute,

Having floated inside the grooved ridges of an old song, a bal
     musette,
The accordion glowing with a waltz.

———

Forget, says a whisper.

———

Tomorrow I must write: *I wish to rest like wind lost in the loose
     boughs of a weeping willow.*

49

Night fell hours ago.
But the wind is still here, and then the forgetting of it.

You had dozed off in a red chair.
I kept looking out the window and wondered,
Now that we are at war,
If even eternity will come to an end,

And we are to become enemies of the state,
Tarred and paraded through town,
Our counterfeit bodies dropped off in dirt lanes.

————

It is not upon you alone the dark patches fall,
The dark threw patches down upon me also—says Walt
    Whitman—
The best I had done seem'd to me blank and suspicious,
My great thoughts, as I supposed them, were they not in reality
    meagre?

Yes, but I must press on about the ghost and the doorknobs—
And the screech of a train between the austere hills—
Until sunlight is everywhere.

Though one day I will no longer remember
This room at all, nothing, or all that I've carried.

And already I am forgetting the sky scrolling east to west.
There's no stopping it.

———

Black smoke was coming out of the North Tower.
Across Liberty Street people were walking through the fallen
   office papers and debris, and the underside of their shoes
   crackling on tiny metal pieces.
Between Deutsche Bank and a firehouse, there was no phone
   reception.
It didn't make sense, except the urge to run to the dock on the
   Hudson River beside the Mercantile Exchange to catch the
   ferry to Hoboken.
It didn't make sense, the thought of another explosion going
   off, and not being able to hold the thought for long.

50

If you looked up, right then, you'd have seen someone jump
    out of one of the buildings.
Someone says that's the third person they had seen jump.

––––––

Like a needle in a compass.

––––––

Walt Whitman says:
It avails not, time nor place—distance avails not.

51

Tomorrow I must write: *Darkness at night does not support one
side of the battle or the other side, but the darkness of the night,
too, is a blanket of togetherness for love.*

———

As if in reply, Walt Whitman says:
*Flood-tide below me! I watch you face to face!
Clouds of the west—sun there half an hour high—I see you also
face to face.*

———

Somewhere a feather scurries over the sky.
Delicate bones, floating away.

Over the empty boulevard below the wind,
A crow glides among the dead and does not bow its head.

52

Every time I look in the mirror now I am like a man returning
    from war,
And it's like I have not seen myself since the refugee camp.

The mirror does not flatter.
There is just whatever looks back,
A face I do not show the others.

I ask, is it time to bid farewell to the half sleep that abides like
    a gray pond under my eyes?
Is it time to say goodbye to the checkpoints, the ID stations,
    the guard shouting, *Hands above your head! Walk slowly*
    backward!

———

Each morning this mirror is a long hallway of black doors,
And running my hand, like a blind man, along the walls,
I unlock the door to the room where last winter's rains are
    forgotten,
And then close the door to turn back down the gray floors,
Stopping again, running back up.

Here I am, like an invisible man, with my smithereens
of faces.

53

Tomorrow I must write: *Is the story ready to be returned and
    shared with others?*

————

I smear the ink on my fingers.
The words coo like doves in the last light.

What is memory but a blue marble
Squeezed into the hand of a little boy dressed for bed?

————

In this room, in this great city, as if from my mouth,
Comes music from a pair of violins and cellos.
Then, like a faint bird, an oboe.

54

What remains is a candle left burning in the window so that
people can see the new trench inching up in the dark.

————

We are tailor-made to step over what comes under our feet.

————

You ask—after all that, why does one fight to love?
Because people want to love.

ACKNOWLEDGMENTS

This is the fourth book of poems of mine brought to you by the University of Washington Press. During these last fifteen years, Linda Bierds has been my guide. To have her literary intellect as my editor is a privilege, and I have been an especially fortunate beneficiary of her comradeship and friendship.

I'm grateful to the Lannan Foundation for support in the writing of this book.

Excerpts from *Republic Café* originally appeared in *American Poetry Review*, *Connotation Press: An Online Artifact*, and *Partisan*.

"Room" was first published in *Poetry*.

ABOUT THE AUTHOR

MARRION ETTLINGER

David Biespiel was born in 1964 in Tulsa and grew up in Houston. He has written five books of poetry, most recently *Charming Gardeners* and *The Book of Men and Women*, which was named one of the Best Books of the Year by the Poetry Foundation. His nonfiction includes the memoir *The Education of a Young Poet*, named by *Poets & Writers* as a Best Book for Writers, and a collection of essays, *A Long High Whistle*, which received the Francis Fuller Victor Award. He writes the Poetry Wire column for *The Rumpus* and is a contributor to *American Poetry Review*, the *New York Times*, *New Republic*, *Poetry*, *Politico*, and *Slate*. He was a finalist for the National Book Critics Circle Balakian Award. Among his honors are a National Endowment for the Arts Fellowship in Literature and a Lannan Fellowship. He is poet-in-residence at Oregon State University, a core faculty member in the Rainier Writing Workshop, and the founder of the Attic Institute of Arts and Letters.

ALSO BY DAVID BIESPIEL

POETRY

Charming Gardeners
The Book of Men and Women
Wild Civility
Pilgrims & Beggars
Shattering Air

NONFICTION

The Education of a Young Poet
A Long High Whistle
Every Writer Has a Thousand Faces

ANTHOLOGIES

Poems of the American South
Long Journey: Contemporary Northwest Poets

RECORDINGS

Citizen Dave: Selected Poems, 1996–2010